TABLE OF CONTENTS

El Salvador

DISCOVER EL SALVADOR CULTURE, SPORTS, HISTORY, CUISINE, LANDMARKS, PEOPLE, TRADITIONS AND MANY MORE FOR KIDS

....

....

ABOUT EL SALVADOR

El Salvador is a smallest country In Central America.

Most people speak Spanish here.

Country currency Salvadoran colón .but they also use U.S Dollar

In 1821 they gained independence from Spain.

"El Salvador" means "The Savior" –in Spanish.

People called Salvadorans.

Population around 6 Million People.

Capital - San Salvador.

El Salvador is also called the "Land of Volcanoes.

They love dance particularly cumbia and salsa music.

GEOGRAPHY

Shared the border with Guatemala, Honduras and Pacific Ocean

El Salvador there are 300 rivers.

23 Active Volcanoes in El Salvador

Lake Coatepeque - it look like a volcano.

Highest Peak - Cerro El Pital.

They country has lot of Eco systems from forests to wetlands.

Longest river- Lempa River

El Tunco and El Sunzal are famous beaches.

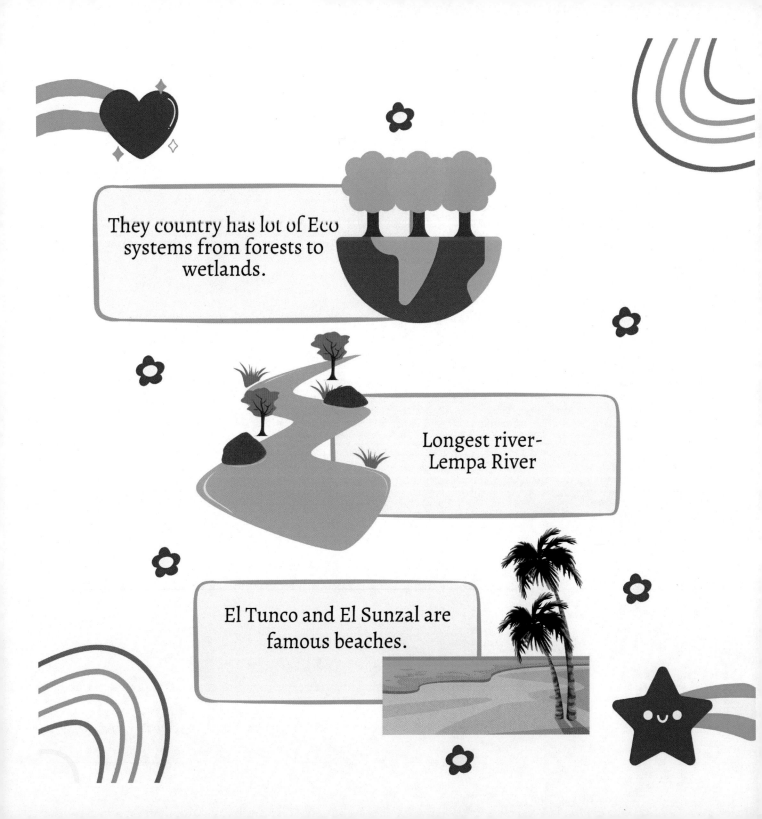

NATIONAL SYMBOLS

National bird Turquoise-browed Motmot or Torogoz

National flower is the "Flor de Izote".

National Flag- blue and white strips with coat of arms in center.

Blue strips represent the Oceans. Like pacific oceans and Caribbean Sea.

Coat of arms represent volcanoes and triangle represent geography of the country.

National tree - Maquilishuat tree.

National anthem-"Himno Nacional de El Salvador."

Motto - "Dios, Unión, Libertad," meaning "God, Union, Liberty."

WEATHER

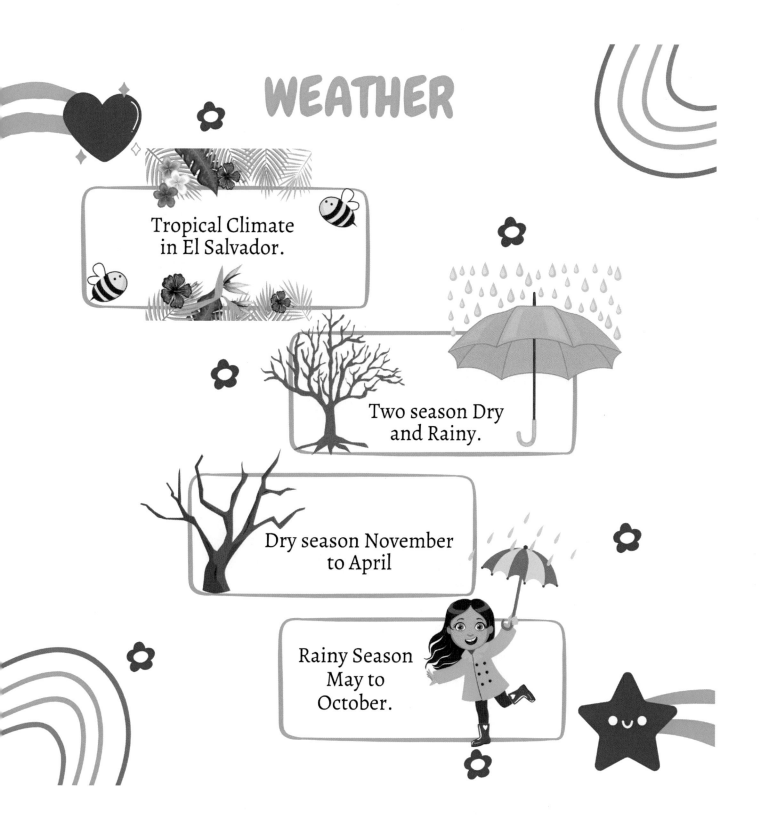

Tropical Climate in El Salvador.

Two season Dry and Rainy.

Dry season November to April

Rainy Season May to October.

Coastal areas to be hotter and mountainous regions are cooler.

The average temperature – in capital -23°C (73°F).

Morning Fogs are very common in mountainous regions.

CONSTITUTION

Constitution was adopted in 1983.

It gives guarantees freedom of speech and religion.

It is a demographic republic.

President is the head of the government and also the state.

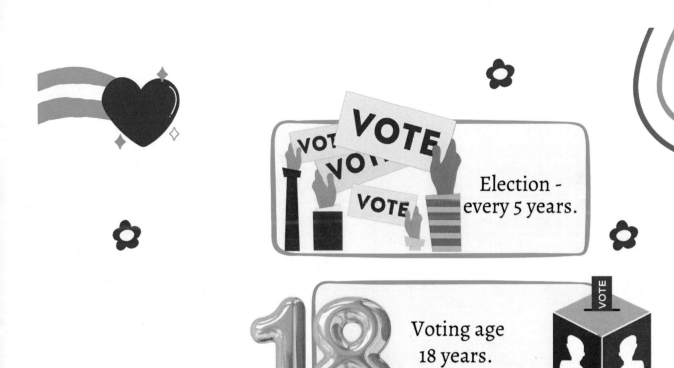

Election - every 5 years.

Voting age 18 years.

National flag was adopted on May 27, 1912. independence day sept 15.

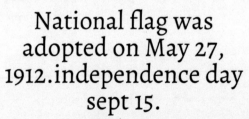

NATIVE ANIMALS

El Salvador jungles u can see lot of animals.

Pocket Gopher

Ocelots.

Sea Turtles and Olive Ridley Turtle

Howler Monkeys

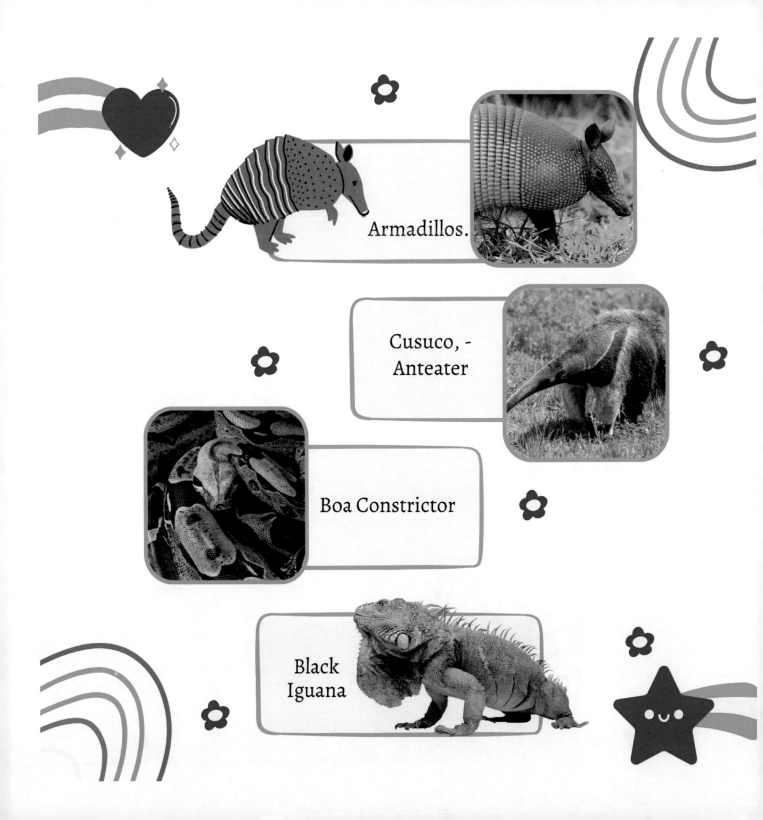

Armadillos.

Cusuco, -
Anteater

Boa Constrictor

Black
Iguana

NATIVE PLANTS

El Salvador Forest you can see lot of trees and Plants.

Maquilishuat tree

Izote flower

 Yucca plant

 Balsam tree- produces a fragrant resin

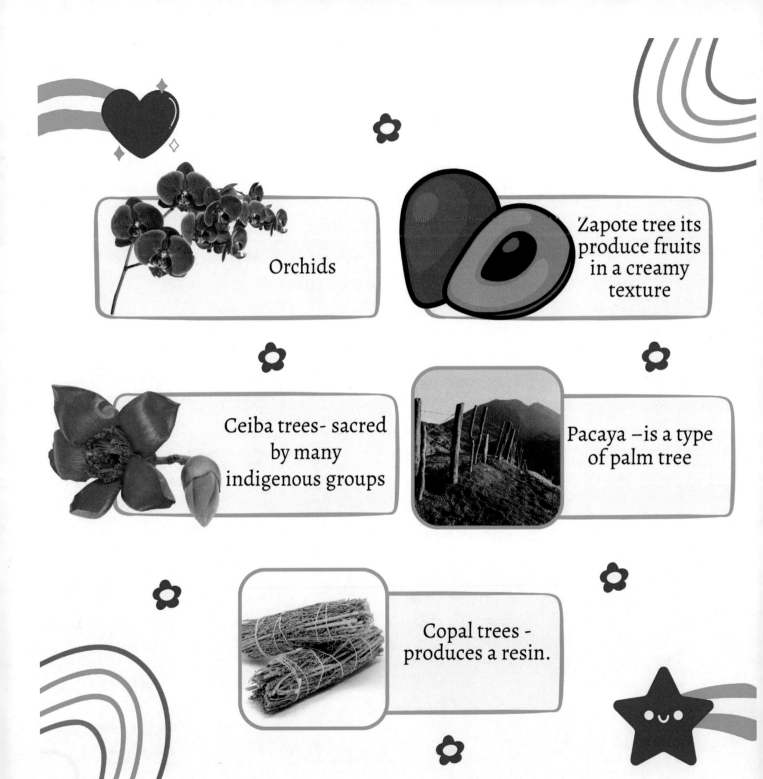

Orchids

Zapote tree its produce fruits in a creamy texture

Ceiba trees- sacred by many indigenous groups

Pacaya –is a type of palm tree

Copal trees - produces a resin.

FAMOUS PEOPLE

Roque Dalton- Poet and activist.

Óscar Romero - saint

Sánchez Cerén –President and guerrilla leader

Maria Isabel Rodriguez – Doctor and public health advocate

Manlio Argueta – novels about Salvadoran life and struggles.

Alfredo Espino –
Poet about nature
and childhood

Carolina
Serrano –
Scientist.

Alvaro Torres –
singer and song
writer

LANDMARKS & ARCHITECTURE

Joya de Cerén UNESCO World Heritage site-preserved under volcano Ash.

Santa Ana Cathedral – Gothic gothic architecture

Tazumal - Mayan archaeological site.

National Palace in San Salvador - neoclassical architecture

Divine Savior of the World - iconic statue in San Salvador

CULTURE AND CUISINE

Pupusas – Popular dish – major ingredient tortillas stuffed with cheese, beans, or meat.

Day of the Dead (Dia de los Muertos)-time to remember loved ones

They often greet with kiss on the cheek or warm handshake

Corn, beans, and rice – main ingredient for their cuisine

During festival time they love to dance with the help Marimba music.

FESTIVALS AND CELEBRATIONS

August Festival (Fiestas Agostinas) – a weeklong celebration.- for honor of the Divine Savior

Panchimalco Flower & Palm Festival. - Indigenous traditions.

November

November month - National Pupusa Day.

Semana Santa (Holy Week).- a colorful processions.

The Balls of Fire Festival celebrate in Nejapa – throwing flaming balls.

San Miguel Carnival – in November – country biggest celebrations

Coatepeque Lake Festival – boat races and fireworks over the lake.

Day of the Cross- Decorating cross with colorful paper and flowers.

Their coffee is rich flavour and also famous in world wide.

Traditional dress - embroidered dresses and white cotton shirts.

SPORTS

Soccer (football) – National team La Selecta.

Surfing – on beaches like El Tunco and Punta Roca.

Basketball and baseball.

Estadio Cuscatlán- largest stadium in Central America.

juego de palín" (a type of field hockey).- Traditional Sports.

Marathons and cycling events –their recreational activities.

Families enjoying Cycling and biking.

FUN FACTS

The country has No Army after 1992 Civil war.

In roadways you can find wildflowers (Ruta de las Flores).

Pupusas – culture heritage of the nation in 2005.

They celebrate New Year's Eve by eating 12 grapes at midnight.

"Jocote," a tropical fruit.

San Salvador city – moved twice due to volcanic activities.

Pacific coast is also called "Turtle Coast" because lot of turtles nesting there.

El Salvador – only country without Caribbean coastline.

smallest national park - "Walter Thilo Deininger,"

"sopa de pata" - unique soap made by cow feet.

National band – ""La Orquesta Internacional Hermanos Flores," has played for over five decades.

You can find detailed clay figurines in - "Ilobasco"

El Salvador 74 % Population live in urban areas.

People known as "guanacos."

In Some regions people speak" Nahuatl".

People like to drink "Kolashampan"an orange colored beverage.

Salvadorans like music particularly cumbia.

First country legalise bitcoin. June 2021

During civil war 1979 to 1992 we lost 80,000 people.

Three million Salvadorans live in United States, largely in Los Angeles.

19% people earn less than $1.25 a day.

San Salvador only 20 miles away from Pacific Ocean.

In 2015 the largest pretzel made in El Salvador, weight 1728 pounds.in 2015.

Excellent destination for bird watching.

The country has rich Mayan history.

It is a cheap travel destination.

You can find a lot of pyramids in El Salvador.

In wild life you can find 800 species.

1970 FIFA world cup qualifiers, El Salvador and Honduras fought war for football.

Made in the USA
Las Vegas, NV
26 November 2024

12729778R00021